LADY J
Covert
FLINT
Warrant Officer
LIFELINE
Rescue Trooper
FROSTBITE
Snow Cat Driver
ROADBLOCK
Heavy Machine Gunner
MAINFRAME
Computer Specialist
WILD BILL
Helicopter Pilot

ACTION FORCE

Action Force is the code name for a highly trained rapid deployment specialist mission force. They are selected from the cream of the world's fighting forces.

ACTION BRIEF

To defend human freedom against Cobra, a ruthless organisation determined to rule the world.

ACTION MISSION

To stop Cobra Commander using the space satellites to ruin world communication.

Series 8710 Action Force

Flint's holiday
Return of the dinosaurs
Spy in the Cobra camp
Tomb of the gods
Action Force goes west
The roof of the world

British Library Cataloguing in Publication Data

Simpson, Dick
The roof of the world.
I. Title II. Davies, Robin, *1950-*
III. Series
823'.914[J]

ISBN 0-7214-1102-9

First edition

Published by Ladybird Books Ltd Loughborough Leicestershire UK
Ladybird Books Inc Auburn Maine 04210 USA

Printed in England

ACTION FORCE™

INTERNATIONAL HEROES

THE ROOF OF THE WORLD

by Dick Simpson
illustrated by Robin Davies

Ladybird Books

Doctor Copernicus, the world famous astronomer, was leading an expedition to find an ancient, mysterious temple.

The monks who had built it were skilled astronomers. From their mountain top they had the best place on earth to observe the stars.

Iceberg, on leave from Action Force to act as cold weather expert to the expedition, spoke. "I'm worried," he said. "The porters are uneasy. They say that

the ancient gods of the mountain still guard the temple. There are also strange creatures seen up here from time to time."

"I know," said the doctor, impatiently. "They call it the roof of the world. They imagine a monster behind every rock."

An hour later they saw a rocky crag rising straight up from a wide snow field. Clinging to the top of the crag was a fantastic building.

"At last!" cried Doctor Copernicus. "Tomorrow I will have my equipment set up in the ruins."

Iceberg studied the building through his binoculars. "There's nothing ruined about it," he said. "It looks in very good shape."

"Nonsense," said the doctor. "The last monk left over a thousand years ago."

"Then, how do you explain that?" asked Iceberg, pointing.

Some distance away, a line of footprints led in the direction of the temple.

Dropping their packs, the porters turned and fled.

"Well, at least we still have our gear," said Iceberg.

He set up the arctic survival tents, prepared a meal, and had a last look at the building on the crag. For a moment he thought he saw a light. "Can't be!" he thought, and crawled into his tent.

* * *

At first light they left the camp. There were more footprints, all leading to the crag.

Iceberg hurried ahead towards a wall of new-looking stone. From behind the wall came a faint humming.

* * *

Left by himself, the doctor decided to do some exploring. He walked along the foot of the crag until he reached a place where all the strange footprints came together.

There was a sound from the rock, and part of it slid aside to reveal a brightly lit tunnel and two white clad figures brandishing weapons.

They seized the doctor and hurried him along the tunnel, while the door slid shut behind them.

Then they were carried swiftly upwards in a lift to a high chamber filled with electronic equipment.

"Welcome, Doctor Copernicus," hissed a sinister voice.

Cobra Commander stepped forward.

* * *

As soon as Iceberg discovered that the doctor was missing, he radioed Action Force Base.

A few hours later, an Action Force transport plane flew low along a wide valley. The cargo doors opened and a Snow Cat slid out to parachute gently onto the snow. Figures landed close by – Hawk, Lady Jaye, Mainframe, Roadblock and Frostbite.

Iceberg explained the situation.

"This has the look of a Cobra operation," said Hawk, "and our first task is to rescue Doctor Copernicus."

"Look! What's that?" cried Frostbite suddenly.

A tall, clumsy figure was shambling across the snow some way off.

Hawk looked through his binoculars. "I don't believe it," he cried. "It's a yeti!"

"All the footprints point to the old temple," said Iceberg. "Cobra Commander must have added yetis to his army."

Action Force piled onto the Snow Cat. Keeping under cover as long as he could, Frostbite brought them in sight of the temple.

"Iceberg," said Hawk, "take Lady Jaye and Roadblock, and check out the spot where the doctor disappeared. The rest of us will take a look from the other side."

As the Snow Cat disappeared, there was a muffled sound of feet crunching in the snow. Less than twenty yards away the hairy bulk of a yeti lumbered towards the crag and the mysterious temple.

"Look at that!" cried Roadblock.

"Quiet!" whispered Iceberg.

But the yeti didn't seem to have heard.

"Are yetis deaf?" said Roadblock.

"Let's see if they are blind, too," said Iceberg. He stood up and waved his arms. The yeti paid no attention.

Lady Jaye unslung her crossbow and loaded the climbing rope and grapnel. She fired, and the rope shot between the yeti's legs, bringing it down with a thump.

Its legs still moved in a walking action. Roadblock leapt on top of it. There was a loud click. The yeti stopped moving.

"I've switched it off!" cried Roadblock.

"It's a primitive robot," said Iceberg. "Programmed to walk about frightening people, and to return to the temple at night. There are probably more of them around."

Meanwhile, the others had reached the far side of the crag. Inside the temple, Cobra Commander watched them on a video screen. "I suppose it was too much to expect Action Force to keep their noses out of my business," he hissed. "If you expect to be rescued, Doctor, you are going to be disappointed."

"What do you want with me?" asked Doctor Copernicus.

"Your brains!" replied Cobra Commander. "I need your expertise. From this place I intend to observe every space satellite. I will control them, steal their messages, send false information, spy on the nations of the world. They will be at my mercy."

* * *

At Iceberg's urgent signal, the Snow Cat raced back and pulled up beside the fallen yeti. Mainframe knelt down for a closer look. "A simple computer controls it," he said. "There's a remote control here. Probably opens and closes a door of some sort."

"Then," said Hawk, "our furry friend can get us inside Cobra's temple, if he can open doors."

"Why not find and round up the lot, and take them with us?" said Lady Jaye. "That should cause enough confusion to help us to get to Doctor Copernicus."

"Good thinking," said Hawk.

Racing across the snow on the Snow Cat, Action Force tracked down yeti after yeti. Each was brought down by Lady Jaye's crossbow, immobilised by Roadblock, and its computer readjusted by Mainframe.

That evening two of Cobra's guards looked down from an opening in the rock. "Time for the robot yetis to start homing in," said one. "There's something wrong," said the other.

A solid mass of yetis was marching purposefully towards them. The hidden door in the rock slid open. The yetis tramped inside, but instead of automatically switching off, they kept on

going. The guards were knocked to the floor, and confusion broke out in the tunnel.

"Now!" cried Hawk.

Action Force sprang from hiding and rushed into the tunnel. Ducking and dodging among the uncontrolled robots, they made for the lift.

An alarm sounded in the temple, but too late! The lift doors sprang open and Hawk burst out, followed by other members of Action Force.

"Don't move!" cried Hawk. "Doctor Copernicus... over here!"

Cobra Commander flicked a hidden switch and everything went dark. Hawk spoke urgently into his handset. "Hawk to Frostbite... NOW!"

Down below the crag, Frostbite fired Snow Cat's missile launcher. With a crash, part of the temple roof was blown away. A flare rocket filled the temple with dazzling light, sending Cobra's men diving for cover.

Cobra Commander shouted, "Stand by... Operation Batwing!"

With a whirr of rotors, a swarm of F.A.N.G. gyrocopters appeared against the night sky. Rope ladders dropped down, and the defeated Cobra force was quickly winched out of reach. Last to leave, Cobra Commander pressed a switch on a panel as he made his retreat.

Hawk found Doctor Copernicus hiding behind a heap of wreckage. Roadblock helped him to his feet. A shout came from Lady Jaye.

"Hawk! The switch Cobra Commander pressed! It's marked 'Self Destruct'!"

"Let's move!" said Hawk. He spoke again into his handset.

"Stand clear!" signalled Frostbite from below in the Snow Cat, as he fired a barrage of rockets trailing ropes and grappling hooks.

In seconds, the Action Force

team was abseiling down the rock face, Doctor Copernicus clinging, eyes tight shut, to Roadblock.

As the loaded Snow Cat raced away from the crag there was the roar of an explosion. Looking back, Doctor Copernicus said, "Look! The temple is a ruin once more! Just as I expected to find it in the first place!"

COBRA ENEMY

COBRA
Cobra Troopers

COBRA COMMANDER

SNOW SERPENT
Cobra Polar Assault

VIPER
Cobra Infantry

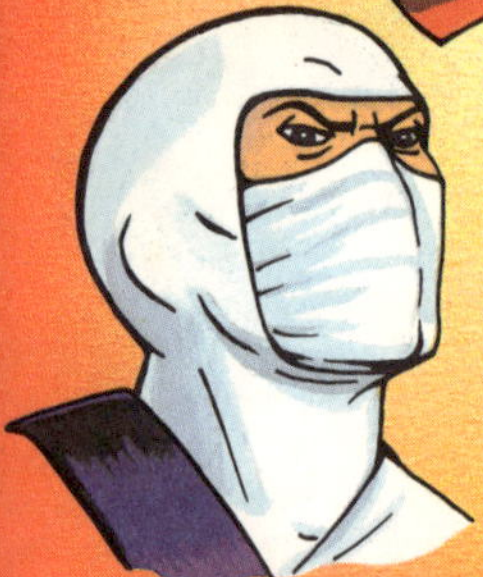

STORM SHADOW
Cobra Ninja

DR MINDBENDER
Master of Mind Control